How to be Born Again & Avoid Hell

DAG HEWARD-MILLS

Parchment House

HOW TO BE BORN AGAIN AND AVOID HELL

Copyright © 2013 Dag Heward-Mills

Originally published 2013 under the title :
The Greater Love of Jesus Christ by Parchment House

ISBN 13: 978-9988-8550-1-7

This edition published 2014 by Parchment House
18th Printing 2018

77Find out more about Dag Heward-Mills at:

Healing Jesus Campaign
Write to: evangelist@daghewardmills.org
Website: www.daghewardmills.org
Facebook: Dag Heward-Mills
Twitter: @EvangelistDag

ISBN : 978-9988-8569-5-3

Contents

CHAPTER 1

God Loves You with a Greater Love

This is my commandment, That ye love one another, as I have loved you. GREATER LOVE HATH NO MAN THAN THIS, that a man lay down his life for his friends. Ye are my friends, if ye do whatsoever I command you.

John 15:12-14

The great love of God will change your life forever. This love is greater than anything found on earth. When a man says to a woman, "I love you", it cannot be compared to the greater love that I am writing about in this book. Your mother may love you, your father may love you; but none of them will die for you. Your boyfriend may love you and your girlfriend may love you, but none will die for you.

This book is about the greater love of God. When you open up your heart to receive this great love, you will be born again. If you open up your heart to this great love from God, you will become a new creation and live a totally different life. If you open up your heart to this great love from God, you will escape your punishment in Hell. You deserve to go to Hell and so do I. But through the love of God who sent His only Son that we might not perish, we can be born again! Hallelujah! We can become new creatures! We can escape the outer darkness and the torments of Hell. What manner of love is this that we can be called the children of God? What great salvation has been shown to us that Jesus should shed His blood to save us from our sins!

I want you to open up your heart and enjoy the great salvation that Christ offers to you. I am sad to say that many Christians do not understand salvation. That is why I am writing this book. Salvation is rarely preached about these days. It is time for us to bring back the solid foundations on which Christianity will forever stand.

Seven Things You Should Know about Greater Love

1. There are different kinds of love, but Jesus' love is the greatest.

God has a special kind of love which is the greatest kind of love in existence. Just look at these Scriptures which describe God's love. What manner of love is this?

God's love is the great love, the everlasting love and the greater love.

Behold, what MANNER OF LOVE the Father hath bestowed upon us, that we should be called the sons of God: therefore the world knoweth us not, because it knew him not.

1 John 3:1

But God, who is rich in mercy, FOR HIS GREAT LOVE wherewith he loved us, even when we were dead in sins, hath quickened us together with Christ, (by grace ye are saved;)

Ephesians 2:4-5

And we have known and believed THE LOVE THAT GOD HATH TO US. God is love; and he that dwelleth in love dwelleth in God, and God in him. Herein is our love made perfect, that we may have boldness in the day of judgment: because as he is, so are we in this world.

1 John 4:16-17

The LORD hath appeared of old unto me, saying, Yea, I have loved thee with AN EVERLASTING LOVE: therefore with lovingkindness have I drawn thee.

Jeremiah 31:3

The Beloved and the Greater Love

I once knew a young lady who had a beloved. This beloved young man wanted to marry the young lady but he did not treat her well. He seemed to be torn between his beloved and some other girls. Their relationship was tumultuous, to say the least. One day, this young lady finally came home and said, "It's over." She was tearful because her heart was broken by the broken relationship. But I comforted her and told her that God would give her somebody else, an even better beloved.

After some months God answered our prayers and a nice young man came out of nowhere and fell in love with her. They seemed to be enjoying their relationship and one day I asked the young lady, "How is your new relationship?"

She smiled and said, "It's far greater than the first relationship. God has been good to me."

In other words, she was experiencing a greater love and a better relationship. So I asked her, "Why is this relationship better?"

She said, "I didn't even know that this is how happy I could be. I didn't know there was a much greater love that I could experience."

Indeed, this young lady experienced a greater kind of love. This is how God's love is. It is a far greater kind of love. What manner of love is this?

2. The love of Jesus is greater than 'the love of brothers'.

Seeing ye have purified your souls in obeying the truth through the Spirit UNTO UNFEIGNED LOVE OF THE BRETHREN, see that ye love one another with a pure heart fervently.

1 Peter 1:22

Many families have disintegrated despite the fact that they are related. They break up and fight each other time and time again. The love of Jesus must be far greater than the love between brethren.

The Kidney Donation

One day, there was a prayer meeting in which prayers were offered up for a brother who needed a kidney donation.

They declared their love for this brother and wanted him to continue to live through a kidney donation.

However, as the prayer meeting went on, they realised that no one was prepared to donate his kidney even though that was what they were praying about. Finally, the leader of the prayer meeting decided to allow God to choose whose kidney should be donated.

So he took a feather and told the gathering that he was going to throw the feather in the air and whoever it landed on would have to donate his kidney. Everyone agreed to this process of divine selection.

He threw the feather in the air. Up it went and came sailing down, amazingly, in the direction of the leader himself. Suddenly, the leader began to shout and blow at the feather so that it would not come to him. It was evident that no one was prepared to donate his kidney; not even the leader. It is one thing to say you love someone but it is another thing to have the "greater love" which makes you sacrifice yourself for him.

3. The love of Jesus is greater than the love of women.

Many songs have been written about the love of women. Actually, most songs are written about the love between men and women and yet much of the pain in the world comes from the break-up of the relationships between men and women. Oh, how easily the love of women goes sour! The love I am writing about is the greater love.

I am distressed for thee, my brother Jonathan: very pleasant hast thou been unto me: THY LOVE TO ME WAS WONDERFUL, PASSING THE LOVE OF WOMEN.

2 Samuel 1:26

AND JACOB LOVED RACHEL; and said, I will serve thee seven years for Rachel thy younger daughter. And Laban said, It is better that I give her to thee, than that I should give her to another man: abide with me.

And Jacob served seven years for Rachel; and they seemed unto him but a few days, for the love he had to her

Genesis 29:18-20

AND THE KING LOVED ESTHER ABOVE ALL THE WOMEN, and she obtained grace and favour in his sight more than all the virgins; so that he set the royal crown upon her head, and made her queen instead of Vashti.

Esther 2:17

The love of women is the love of the female body; with this kind of love the woman gives her body to a man to indulge him. The love of women is short-lived. Most women are unable to keep the attention of a man for very long. I had a friend who had two girlfriends. I asked him how he could have two girlfriends at the same time. Then he answered, "I used to have eight girlfriends when I was in sixth form but now that I am in the university I have only two." This young man had a very short attention span for the different women in his life. The love of Jesus lasts longer than the lust a man has for different women.

The love of Jesus has lasted throughout the centuries. It has persisted until it reached you and me. The love of Jesus Christ is a far greater kind of love than the love a man can have for a woman.

There are limitations with this love of women. Even the most intense couples need counselling shortly after they are married. Many who say "I love you"; "You're my dream"; "I'm so happy I met you" will often say the same things to another person. Obviously there is something missing in this "love for women".

The Widow

There was a certain pastor who lived happily with his wife until he died unexpectedly. The wife was heartbroken and she cried continually.

Her pastor tried to counsel her but she could not be comforted.

One day, she went to the graveside and wept from morning to evening. As she cried she scratched and clawed at the grave. She wanted to pull her husband out of the grave.

One day, the pastor had a vision and he was taken to Heaven where he saw the husband of this lady. To his amazement, this man was very happy in Heaven. He spoke to the pastor and told him that he was very happy to be in Heaven. The pastor told him, "Your wife is crying every day and she cannot be comforted."

Then the dead pastor told him something truly shocking. He said, "Oh, don't worry about my wife. The Lord told me when I got here that she was going to be okay and that He was even going to give her a new husband who would be better than me."

He said, "Please tell my wife when you go that this is what the Lord said."

"But she won't believe me."

"Don't worry, the pastor said, I will tell you a secret between her and me. When you tell her she will know that you have spoken to me."

Then the dead husband told him a secret that only he and his wife knew.

After the vision, the pastor called this woman and told her that he had seen her husband and that she was going to have a new husband who would be better than the old one.

She said, "No way, it can never happen. I will never have a new husband and no one could be better than my husband."

Then he told her the secret. She screamed and said, "You have been standing outside our window to listen to our conversation."

It was then that she realised that it was a real vision.

As time passed she did marry again. One day the pastor asked her, "How is your new marriage?"

She smiled sheepishly and said, "Indeed this new husband is far greater than my first husband. I am experiencing a greater love."

This lady experienced greater love in her second marriage. Indeed, there are lesser and greater kinds of love but Jesus' love is a far greater love than the love of women or the love of brethren.

4. The love of Jesus is greater than the love of a nation.

People claim to love their countries. But when the country is poor, they claim citizenship of another country if they can. A lot of Ghanaians and Nigerians have changed their nationalities and are now proud to be British, American, Italian and German citizens. People change their accents and dissociate from their countries at the slightest opportunity. But Jesus Christ stayed by His cross and died for the whole world. The love of Jesus Christ is far greater than the love anyone can have for his country.

5. The love of Jesus is greater than the love of a mother for her children.

Can a woman forget her sucking child, that she should not have compassion on the son of her womb? Yea, they may forget, yet will I not forget thee.

Isaiah 49:15

Mothers can and do forget their children. Some mothers drop their children on the doorstep of another and turn away forever. Indeed, the love of a mother is a great thing to behold. But it cannot be compared to the greater love that Jesus exhibited when He gave up His life for the whole world.

6. The love of Jesus is greater love because He sacrificed Himself for us.

This love is greater because one usually gives something when he loves. Jesus did not give us money, houses or cars as some do; He laid down his life! He gave His life; He did not live to be seventy years.

He poured out His blood for us. The blood is the life. He gave us His life by giving His blood.

HEREBY PERCEIVE WE THE LOVE OF GOD, because he laid down his life for us: and we ought to lay down our lives for the brethren.

1 John 3:16

And from Jesus Christ, who is the faithful witness, and the first begotten of the dead, and the prince of the kings of the earth. UNTO HIM THAT LOVED US, AND WASHED US from our sins IN HIS OWN BLOOD.

Revelation 1:5

The Man in the Deep Freezer

One day, a young man met a lady and told her how much he loved her. This young lady was enthralled by the love the young man showered on her and decided to marry him. They got married, moved into their new house and bought furniture, a deep freezer, a fridge and all the things they needed to make a happy home.

One night, they were in bed when armed robbers broke into the house. The husband managed to escape into the living room and did not know where to go next. When he saw the new empty deep freezer, an idea occurred to him to jump into it and hide in it. When the armed robbers could not find him, they beat up his wife and maltreated her. As the wife screamed and called for help the husband was nowhere to be found because he was hiding in the deep freezer. When the armed robbers finally left, he came out of the deep freezer to console his wife. But she would have none of it.

"You don't love me," she said. "If you had loved me you would have come out of the deep freezer to save me."

The husband said, "I love you but not that much."

Then he continued, "Don't you understand? There is nothing much that I could have done. Those guys would have killed me. I would have lost my life trying to save you.

I would have been a hero but I would have lost my life."

Later on when the lady went to church, she heard the pastor preaching, "Greater love hath no man than this that a man lay down his life for his friends."

Then she realized that her husband had been unable to lay down his life for her. Even though he did love her to an extent, her husband's love could not be compared with the love that Jesus had for her. Jesus Christ laid down His life for her. Her husband did not do that.

7. You shall not escape if you neglect such a great love.

To ignore, to despise and to neglect the greater love of Jesus is to leave yourself to suffering and unhappiness. If you reject such great love, I wonder who will love you in future.

How shall we escape, if we neglect so great salvation; which at first began to be spoken by the Lord, and was confirmed unto us by them that heard him;
Hebrews 2:3

The Desperate Beauty

When I was in the university, I knew many beautiful Christian girls. There was this particular Christian girl who was outstandingly beautiful. All the young men wanted to be in a relationship with her and marry her. She received many letters from many young men. She simply read every letter and made fun of the people who had written to her. She would show the letters to her friends and they would have a good laugh. Eventually, she left the university and fewer and fewer young men were interested in her. At a point no one proposed to her anymore.

As the years went by, she became desperate and decided to join a church where the pastor did not have a wife.

After some time she realised that the pastor was not noticing her so she decided to dance in front of him during the praise and worship time. Somehow, he still did not notice her.

Eventually, she decided to go and propose to the pastor herself. She went up to him and said, "I would like to marry you. Will you marry me or not?" But he did not want to marry her. How embarrassed she was! What a shame! Someone who was desired by so many people now had no one who loved her and wanted her.

You see, if you reject great love you will one day regret it. A day will come when you will not get such love showered on you. You will live to discover that you cannot escape if you neglect the way of salvation that Jesus brings.

The Grieving Widow

One day, I met a lady whose husband had died. Her husband had been a pastor who had died in his early forties. She told me how her husband loved to pass by her and make swipes.

She said, "Anytime he walked past me at home, he would touch me. But I did not like it. I did not appreciate his constant touching."

She proceeded to tell me about how he had been stricken by cancer in the midst of his years. According to her, a time came when he would lie down at home, unable to raise his hands. She would pass by him, as at other times, but this time he could neither raise his hands nor give her one of his cuddles.

She said, "As he lay there dying I wished so much that he would stretch his hand and touch me like he used to." But it was all over. She had rejected his love many times but wished she could have it again.

The very thing you reject may be the only way by which God will bless you. Open your heart to the greater love of Jesus and enjoy His love, forgiveness and blessing.

CHAPTER 2

Don't Be Surprised That You Must Be Born Again

What Does It Mean to Be Born Again?

There was a man of the Pharisees, named Nicodemus, a ruler of the Jews: The same came to Jesus by night, and said unto him, Rabbi, we know that thou art a teacher come from God: for no man can do these miracles that thou doest, except God be with him. Jesus answered and said unto him, Verily, verily, I say unto thee, Except a man be born again, he cannot see the kingdom of God. Marvel not that I said unto thee, Ye must be born again.

John 3:1-3, 7

I n this passage, Jesus had a discussion with a man called Nicodemus. Jesus was at home one night when Nicodemus came to Him. Nicodemus was a very important person in town. The Bible says he was a ruler of the Jews, a master of Israel, a leader in the synagogues. Nicodemus went to see Jesus at night, so that all the people who respected him would not see him.

This prominent Jewish leader said something to Jesus, which prompted Him to give an interesting reply. Nicodemus told Jesus that he recognized Him as a great man of God.

Jesus saw right through him and replied, "You must be born again. You are a good person. I know you pay tithes and fast often. You are a Pharisee, and a ruler of the Jews, but you still need to be born again!"

Now, the questions we have to ask ourselves are these:

"Why did Jesus tell Nicodemus that he had to be born again?"

"Why did He launch out into this sermon?"

The word "born" means "to be produced or created". Therefore, to be "born again" means "to be produced or created again".

There are lots of people doing all sorts of religious things. These religious activities make people look like and feel that they are Christians, but actually they are not. Being religious does not make you born again. Such people are not born again.

Indeed, apart from Christianity there is no religion that requires a person to be born or created again. All the major religions of this world give instructions for their followers to obey. There is, however, no religion that claims an inner new birth. Christianity stands alone in this claim!

To understand what it means to be born again, we can look at what being born again is not! To understand the Bible better, I often try to look at the opposite of what is written. This can be very revealing.

For example: "...Seek ye first the Kingdom of God, and his righteousness; and all these things shall be added unto you" (Matthew 6:33). The opposite of this is: "...Do not seek first the Kingdom of God, and all these things shall not be added unto you." It is as simple as that.

If you do not seek first the Kingdom of God, you cannot expect God to give you the things you need.

So, to understand the concept of being born again, we are going to look at twenty things that are NOT the same as being born again.

Twenty Things That Are Not the Same as Being Born Again

1. Admiring miracles is not the same as being born again.

Whenever there is a miracle worker, large crowds gather. These crowds are often not stable crowds; they only gather for a reason and for a season. The large crowds who gather to experience miracles are not necessarily born again.

When Jesus himself organized miracle crusades, large crowds gathered but when he began teaching certain hard truths, he was deserted by all, except the twelve disciples (John 6). A deep admiration for miracles is not the same as being born again.

2. Befriending a man of God is not the same as being born again.

Nicodemus got acquainted with Jesus and became His friend. In the same way, there are many who have become friends of pastors and men of God. Jesus did not say, "Except a man has a pastor as his friend...." He did say, "...except a man be born again he cannot see the Kingdom of God" (John 3:3).

3. Giving money to a church is not the same as being born again.

Giving money to a church is not the same as being born again. Some people have given money to churches for many years, but that is not a substitute for being born again. It will not result in the giver receiving special treatment at the gates of Heaven. Though it is good to give to God, no matter how much money you contribute to the church, you still need to be born again.

4. Joining a church is not the same as being born again.

A person may join a church by registering as a member of that church and still not be born again. I have been in church all my life but I did not get born again until I was a teenager. In "religious" countries such as many African countries, you could easily be a member of a church, and not be born again.

5. Playing a role in a church is not the same as being born again.

It is possible to play a prominent role in church without being born again. For instance, during an altar call in our church, some choristers responded to the call to give their lives to Christ. They were members of the choir, but were not born again Christians. A person who is not born again may get involved in church activities and even become a priest. There are priests standing behind the "sacred desks" in many churches who are not born again! Playing a role in church is not the same as being born again.

6. Praying every day is not the same as being born again.

Praying every day is not the same as being born again. When I was a child, I approached a priest and asked him, "Sir, how can I go to Heaven?"

He said, "My son, pray 'Hail Mary' three times a day, and 'Our Father' once a day, and you will go to Heaven."

I thanked him, and began to pray every day, reciting The Lord's Prayer and Hail Mary.

Oh, how I prayed! But, that was not the way to salvation! I diligently followed my priest's instructions but I was still not born again.

You may be very religious, but if you are not born again, you will die and go to Hell.

7. Reading the Bible is not the same as being born again.

Reading the Bible and quoting the Scriptures is not a guarantee of salvation. You may be able to quote the Bible from Genesis to Revelation. This does not mean that you are born again. There are theologians who have degrees in all sorts of theological studies, but are not born again.

8. Being baptized is not the same as being born again.

Baptism is not the same as being born again. Jesus Himself commanded us to be baptized, but He said baptism should follow salvation.

Go ye into all the world, and preach the gospel to every creature. He that believeth and is baptized shall be saved...

Mark 16:15, 16

You have to believe before you are baptized. It has become some people's tradition to baptize little babies when they are a few days old. How can you believe when you are eight days old?

Baptism is immersion in water: a sign to the person being baptized and to all witnesses that he is now born again. The "old man" of sin goes down into the water and the "new man" recreated in Christ emerges.

We know that baptism is a sign of what has happened on the inside. This is because when you are born again, nothing actually happens physically for those around to see. So, being baptized becomes a physical sign of what happened inside but is not the same as being born again.

9. Being "confirmed" in a church is not the same as being born again.

In some churches, a person is baptized by the sprinkling of water on him when he is a few days old.

It is expected that when he grows up he will come back to the church to confirm his Christianity. This is what is known as "confirmation".

I think that what really happened is this: At some point in the development of Christianity, people felt that they were "big-shots", too big to be immersed publicly in water. It was humiliating for them to be put into water publicly, so I believe it was arranged for people to be baptized as children. Then, when they grew up, they were confirmed. The result of this has been the creation of a large sea of confirmed sinners and unbelievers who are deceived that they are born again. Being confirmed is not the same as being born again.

10. Taking Holy Communion is not the same as being born again.

Taking Holy Communion is not the same as being born again. It does not matter how much of the communion wine you drink, or how much of the bread you eat. Taking Holy Communion or the Lord's Supper is actually meant for born-again Christians, who eat the bread and drink the wine in remembrance of Christ's death. However, it is now common to find Reverend Ministers serving communion to die-hard sinners who come to church on special occasions. Pastors also serve Holy Communion to unbelievers who are on their deathbeds, approaching the gates of Hell.

But eating a big loaf of bread and drinking a whole crate of communion wine cannot save your soul and does not make you born again.

11. Being in a Christian family is not the same as being born again.

Being in a Christian family is not the same as being born again. I was brought up in a "Christian" family. I was baptized as a baby, and then confirmed later. I was also given a Bible and a hymn book by my godmother in England, but it just gathered dust on the shelf. I was in the church with my family for years until I became born again. There was a definite point in my life when I got born again.

I find that religious people are surprised (like Nicodemus), when they are told they must be born again. They believe they have been devoted "Christians" all their lives, probably singing all the hymns, songs and doxologies they know.

If some young man comes along to tell such religious people that they need to be born again, you can understand their surprise. Indeed, a "Christian" upbringing is no substitute for being born again.

12. Using Christian jargon is not the same as being born again.

Using Christian jargon is not the same as being born again. Examples of these are: "Praise the Lord", "Hallelujah", "Glory", "Be blessed", and "Amen, brother!"

I have worked with people in various Christian groups. There are times I have felt that some of these people were not really born again. I doubted if they were really Christians, yet they were so rich in Christian jargon. When they met you, they knew exactly what they were supposed to say.

13. Denominationalism is not the same as being born again.

Denominationalism, or "Churchianity", is not the same as being born again. Being a member of one of the great denominations of our day does not make you a born-again Christian.

You may be in the Lighthouse Church, but be an unbeliever. In the same way, you may be in the Methodist Church, but simply be a Methodist unbeliever. The Catholic Church is a very powerful denomination, which I really respect. In my estimation, many churches are not as devoted and as charitable as the Catholic Church. Many Charismatic and Pentecostal pastors have a lot to learn from our Catholic brothers. When I was in the medical school, I had the opportunity to learn first-hand about the

Catholic Relief Services. They offer wonderful social, medical, and relief services. God bless their hearts for all their efforts.

However, it is my duty to inform all Catholics, Methodists, Presbyterians, Baptists, Pentecostals and Lighthouse members that they must be born again. Being part of your great denomination does not mean that you are born again.

14. Being a moralist is not the same as being born again.

Being a moralist is not the same as being born again. There are some people who have very high morals. But having good morals is not the same as being born again.

For instance, there are some people who would never break their marriage vows. I once spoke to an unbeliever, who belonged to an occult group. He told me he had been married for seventeen years but had never been unfaithful to his wife, even though she could not have a child. This is a test many born-again Christians may not be able to pass. Many people go outside their marriages and break their wedding vows in order to have children. But listen, being such a moralist does not mean you are born again.

I congratulate you for your morality. I respect you for the fact that you never commit adultery or fornication. I am glad that you are not into pornography or prostitution, but I must still inform you that you must be born again! Nicodemus was a moralist, that is why he was so surprised when Jesus told him that he needed to be born again. "Marvel not that I said unto thee, Ye must be born again."

15. Being principled is not the same as being born again.

Being a man of principles is not the same as being born again. Some people are very principled and will not cheat you, even if they have the opportunity to do so. Sometimes people cheat in examinations, but such principled people will not have anything to do with it!

I have found it more difficult to bring principled, moral people to Christ. Hard-core sinners are more aware that they need God. A very principled person sees no reason why he must be saved.

His excuse is often, "Why? I am a good person, why should I change?" "Verily I say unto you, That the publicans and the harlots go into the kingdom of God before you" (Matthew 21:31).

There are principled doctors who are not born again, who simply refuse to do abortions. To them, abortion is murder. Yet, even such principled doctors need to be born again.

16. Being respectable is not the same as being born again.

Being respectable is not the same as being born again. Indeed, you may have been respected in society for many years. All your life you may have been singled out and given leadership responsibilities.

Perhaps, you are a person in authority now. You could be the President of a country, a parliamentarian, a Minister of State, a King, a Chief, a headmaster or headmistress. Such positions are held in high esteem. Do not be deceived. That respect accorded you does not mean you are born again. Jesus says to the President, "Marvel not that I said unto thee, Ye must be born again."

17. Being popular is not the same as being born again.

Being popular or famous is not the same as being born again. I remember a particular short young man who was extremely popular in my school. Whenever he walked in or out of any school gathering, there was a great uproar, as everybody cheered him on. He was a very popular guy but he still needed to be born again! You may be popular. People may hail you wherever you go, but you still need to be born again!

Popular politicians need to be born again in spite of their popularity. In spite of their popularity they must still be born again! People may like you. Everybody may be pleased with you. Yet, being popular is not the same as being born again. Marvel not that I say unto you, you must be born again.

18. Obeying a new set of rules is not the same as being born again.

Being born again is not the same as obeying a new set of rules. When you join a club, such as an Old Boys' Association or a Keep Fit Club, you may be presented with a new set of rules. My wife's school, Wesley Girls' High School, had as its motto: "Live pure, Speak true, Right wrong and Follow the King".

This set of rules may be your guiding principle. But you still need to be born again.

There are also people who are rich in wise sayings. In Ghana, one of our popular wise sayings can be translated as, "The animal without a tail is protected by God". The deeper meaning of this is, "God takes care of the fatherless". How wise and impressive this sounds! Another wise saying goes like this: "The old man who is sitting at the foot of the irokko tree sees further than the young man who climbs to the top of the tree." Wow! How wise and how deep! Another wise saying is, "A stranger has eyes but he cannot see." This is fantastic. These sayings are really deep. Such deep wisdom does not mean that you are born again.

Throughout your entire life you may be guided by these nice-sounding wise quotes. However, Jesus says to you, "You must still be born again."

19. Being a good spouse is not the same as being born again.

Being a good wife or a good husband does not mean that a person is born again. You may love your husband, look after him, submit to him, support him and pray for him but it does not mean you are born again. You may be living happily together, but it does not mean you will go to Heaven. Good family people are often surprised when you tell them to be born again.

They will say, "Look at me! What is wrong with me? I am a good person, and this is my happy wife. I have a good life, a good family and nice children. We are living happily ever after! What could be better than that?"

I agree to all that you have said, but you still need to be born again.

20. Being rich or poor is not the same as being born again.

Being rich or poor is not the same as being born again. Being poor in this life is all the more reason why you must be born again. Your poverty and suffering in this life should not deceive you into thinking that there will be peace after death. If you are not born again, your poverty will not save you.

You still need to be born again. Otherwise you will go to Hell and live in torment for eternity.

If you are very rich and everything is going well, you may think you don't need to add anything to your life. Jesus says to the rich and the poor alike, "Marvel not that I said unto thee, Ye must be born again."

In Luke 16:19-31, we read about the rich man. He was a fool, not because he was rich, but because in his rich state he did not acknowledge God. Often, rich people forget about God. Do not be just a rich man; be a wise and rich person.

When the rich man found himself in Hell he became a virtual evangelist urging people to rise from the dead to take the message to his brothers. Mr. Rich Man, do not be surprised that you must be born again. You need to believe in God. You need to believe in Jesus.

CHAPTER 3

What It Means to Be a New Creation

… if anyone is in Christ, he is a new creation…
2 Corinthians 5:17

W hen a man is born again he becomes a new creation. The "new creation" is a term used in the Bible to explain and describe a saved person. It is important to understand what it means to be a new creature in Christ. The concept of being a new creation is simply fascinating. God in His great wisdom has changed our hearts and made us new on the inside. This is very different from the experience of other religions. Most other religions simply have a set of rules they have to follow. We have far more than that! We have the wonderful experience of being recreated in the Spirit.

A new heart also I will give you, and a new spirit will I put within you: and I will take away the stony heart out of your flesh, and I will give you an heart of flesh.

Ezekiel 36:26

The new creation is not a new creation of your body. People who are born again have not changed in their bodies. The new creation is not a renovated old creation. The new creation is not an improved version of the old creation. The new creation is a brand new thing that never existed before. When you are born again, God has put in you a brand new heart and you are a new creature. You have a heart that never existed before. You have a soul that never existed before. You are a new man and new things are about to happen in your life. Praise the Lord!

In this chapter, I want to share about what it means to be a new creature. You must understand what has happened in your life. When a person undergoes surgery, he must understand what has happened to him. Sometimes after surgery, there are certain things you can do and certain things you cannot do. Surgery can change your lifestyle in a dramatic way. When you are born again, you have had spiritual surgery. Actually, you have had spiritual transplant surgery and have been given a new heart. What does this mean for you? What do you need to know about the new creation?

Seven Great Principles about the New Creation

1. Man is a spirit, has a soul and lives in a body.

The fact that a human being is actually a spirit living inside a physical body is one of the lesser known truths. When Paul wrote to the Thessalonians he wrote that God should affect them in all three areas: spirit, soul and body.

And the very God of peace sanctify you wholly; and I pray God your whole SPIRIT and SOUL and BODY be preserved blameless unto the coming of our Lord Jesus Christ.

1 Thessalonians 5:23

A human being is not just a piece of meat. When Princess Diana died many people in this world reflected on the reality of spiritual issues. I - spoke to somebody in the lobby of Novotel Accra. He asked me what I did and I told him that I was a pastor. "Oh, I see," he said.

"Do you believe in God?" I asked him.

"Actually, I had just been thinking about this."

He continued, "When Princess Diana died I wondered whether I was just a piece of meat."

I told him, "You are not just a piece of meat. There is more to you than a piece of meat."

When people speak in a very proud and arrogant way, it is because they are not aware of how real eternal things are. I will never forget my first day as a medical student in the laboratory in the University of Ghana Medical School. It was about 2 o'clock in the afternoon when we were ushered into a large air-conditioned room containing twelve white marble tables. On each of these tables was a dead human being lying stark naked.

There were about ten men and two women. My friends and I gathered around one of the tables. There were stools around each table and I sat down staring at the dead body that lay before me. On the chest of this human being was a plaster with a name inscribed. The name of our cadaver was Cornelius.

I wondered to myself, "Who was Cornelius during his lifetime? What did he do for a living? How did he come to lie before us, ready for eighteen months of intensive dissection?"

As we sat there, our Anatomy lecturer came in. He happened to be a Christian. He said to us, "Go ahead and touch them, don't be afraid!" But in spite of his encouragement, most people were scared by the whole scene.

This anatomy lecturer said something that has stayed with me since then. He said, "This scene should make everyone of you seriously consider what life is all about." He added, "If life just consists of the physical then even goats are better. Because when goats die they can be eaten, but human beings cannot be eaten."

I thought about that statement and I realized that life must consist of more than what we see physically. Man is a spirit. The Bible says that God is the Father of spirits.

...shall we not much rather be in subjection unto the FATHER OF SPIRITS, and live?
Hebrews 12:9

If God is the Father of spirits, then we His children are spirits. That means that our bodies are just containers of the spirit. The Bible describes the body as a house.

For we know that if our EARTHLY HOUSE of this tabernacle were dissolved, we have a building of God, an house not made with hands, eternal in the heavens.
2 Corinthians 5:1

When Lazarus of Luke 16 died, the Bible teaches us that he was carried by the angels into Abraham's bosom.

And it came to pass, that the beggar died, and was carried by the angels into Abraham's bosom...
Luke 16:22

I once passed by an unmarked grave. I saw three men throwing dead bodies into the mass grave. I went up to the car and asked, "What are you doing?"

They were hospital officials who had been sent to bury unclaimed bodies. I immediately remembered Lazarus. These were modern-day Lazaruses. But that is not the end of the story. After the body dies, the spirit lives on.

Lazarus himself, the real man, was carried into Abraham's bosom. Remember also the testimony of the rich man. He had everything in life. He had better health care so he lived longer than Lazarus. However, it came to pass that he also died. He probably had a grand funeral.

Years ago, I attended a funeral of someone. His funeral was very grand. Dignitaries travelled from all over the country to attend the funeral. Special invitation cards were issued for the funeral. The corpse had several changes of clothing during the night. The most amazing part of the funeral was that a new road was actually constructed in the town to enable everybody to attend the funeral in comfort.

I don't know if you are aware of the cost of constructing a road. No expenses were spared for the funeral of this great rich man. This funeral also reminded me of the story of the rich man in the book of Luke. But the story does not end there. The Bible says in Hell he lifted up his eyes. The man still had eyes even though he was in Hell. He cried to Father Abraham that he should allow Lazarus to dip the tip of his finger in water to cool his tongue.

And in hell he lift up his EYES, being in torments, and SEETH Abraham afar off, and Lazarus in his bosom. And he CRIED [mouth/voice] and said, Father Abraham, have mercy on me, and send Lazarus, that he may dip the tip of his FINGER in water and cool my TONGUE; for I am tormented in this flame.

Luke 16:23,24

Notice that different parts of the body have been mentioned. The picture of a man is being painted. This is interesting because the Bible describes the spirit of a man as the hidden man, inward man or the inner man.

Dear friend, the Lazarus who was in Abraham's bosom was not the real Lazarus. It was the soul and spirit of Lazarus. The rich man who was languishing in Hell was not the rich man who had been buried at that lavish funeral. It was the soul and the spirit of the rich man that was experiencing the fires of Hell. You can verify for yourself, whether the body stays in the grave or not! The mortal remains of human beings remain on earth long after the spirit has departed to eternal life or damnation.

I know that many Christians are not aware of this great reality: that they are spirit, soul and body. When many Christians wake up in the morning, they spend a long time bathing, brushing their teeth and getting ready.

Many ladies spend a long time getting ready to go out. After that they may have a good breakfast or lunch before moving out. Then these born-again Christians walk out of the door without even saying a five-minute prayer. This is because they are not aware that they are more than a body. It is only because they are not conscious that they are spirits living in a body that they spend all their time on the body only.

When a person becomes aware of his spirit and soul, he spends time to build up and develop the spirit.

Many governments are not aware that a human being is made up of more than just a body and a mind. They stress education and physical fitness but they leave out the real person. Man is a spiritual being first of all. The mind and the body are just mortal containers of the human spirit.

It is time for Christians to be aware of the spirit that dwells in them. It is time for us to develop the human spirit. You can develop your human spirit by praying.

He that speaketh in an unknown tongue EDIFIETH [builds up, charges] HIMSELF...

1 Corinthians 14:4

The Bible says that when you speak in tongues you build up, charge and edify your spirit. It is good to do bodily exercises. We are not against that! But what about spiritual exercises? Be conscious of your spirit within. You are a spirit, you have a soul and you live in a body.

But what is a soul? The Bible makes it clear that the soul is different from the spirit.

For the word of God is quick, and powerful, and sharper than any twoedged sword, piercing even to the dividing asunder of SOUL and SPIRIT...

Hebrews 4:12

There is a dividing asunder (demarcation) between the spirit and the soul of a man. There are so many words in the Bible that are used to describe the actions of the soul. The soul can be said to be rejoicing (Psalm 31:7). The soul can magnify and bless the Lord (Psalm 103:2). The soul can be downcast (Psalm 42:5). The soul can be grieved (Judges 10:16). The soul can be discouraged (Numbers 21:4). The soul can be joyful (Psalm 35:9).

These are just a few of the emotions that the soul expresses. We can therefore conclude that the soul is the part of the man that experiences thoughts, feelings and emotions.

You will realize that the soul of the rich man was alive in Hell. That is why he could remember Lazarus. The rich man thought things were still the same as when he was alive on earth. That is why he wanted to send Lazarus like a messenger, to come all the way from Heaven to Hell to serve him some water.

The rich man remembered his five brothers and pleaded with Father Abraham to prevent them from coming to join him in Hell. He pitied anyone who would ever come to Hell.

29

The soul of the rich man had perished in the lake of fire and he could remember, think and feel as though he was on earth.

What did Jesus say about the soul? He said, "What shall it profit a man if he shall gain the whole world and lose his soul?" It is the soul that goes to Hell. Your spirit and your soul will suffer in Hell.

For what shall it profit a man, if he shall gain the whole world, and LOSE HIS OWN SOUL?

Mark 8:36

2. **The spirit of an unsaved man is dead and desperately wicked.**

When a person is not born-again he has what I call an unsaved spirit. There are many different ways the Bible describes an unbeliever. The Bible calls a non-Christian an unbeliever, a sinner and unregenerate. It is important for you to be aware of the condition of the human spirit.

The heart [unsaved spirit] is DECEITFUL above all things, and DESPERATELY WICKED: who can know it?

Jeremiah 17:9

But the Word of God makes it abundantly clear that anyone who is not a believer has an unregenerate spirit and is capable of many evil things. The fact that an unsaved man is in a terrible spiritual condition is made abundantly clear in Romans chapter one. The Bible says that God's wrath is being released against the wickedness of men.

For the wrath of God is revealed from heaven against all ungodliness and unrighteousness of men...

Romans 1:18

The human race has forsaken the living God and therefore God has given them up to become dead and darkened in their spirits.

When they knew God, they glorified him not as God, neither were thankful; become vain in their imaginations, AND THEIR FOOLIŚH HEART WAS DARKENED.

Romans 1:21

The heart of the unsaved person is darkened and degenerate. God has gone a step further and given up mankind so that they may follow their own desires and perverted feelings.

Wherefore GOD ALSO GAVE THEM UP TO UNCLEANNESS through the lusts of their own hearts, to dishonour their own bodies between themselves.

Romans 1:24

Not only is the spirit of the unsaved man darkened with death but the mind of the unsaved human race has also degenerated into a depraved condition.

...and even as they did not like to retain God in their knowledge, GOD GAVE THEM OVER TO A REPROBATE MIND to do those things which are not convenient.

Romans 1:28

As you read this passage further, you will discover that the sinful human race is filled with every conceivable evil. The long list of evil characteristics is there for your reading.

Being filled with all unrightcousness, fornication, wickedness, covetousness maliciousness; full of envy, murder, debate, deceit, malignity; whisperers, Backbiters, haters of God, despiteful, proud, boasters, inventors of evil things, disobedient to parents, Without understanding, covenantbreakers, without natural affection, implacable, unmerciful:

Romans 1:29-31

This principle that an unsaved spirit is desperately wicked is manifest every day of our lives. God has warned against marrying non-Christians because a non-Christian has an unregenerate spirit and is capable of many evil things. One of the things that an unbeliever is filled with is covenant breaking (Romans 1:31).

Most unbelievers do not stick to their word. It is rare to find an unbeliever who is faithful to his marriage covenant. One man told me, "I have never seen a faithful unbeliever husband before."

As I grew up in life I came to discover that covenant breaking was part and parcel of the unbeliever's lifestyle. They say, "I will" and "I do", but they won't and they don't. This is the reason why God says Christians should not marry unbelievers. Do not think that God is trying to punish you by telling you not to marry an unbeliever. God is trying to prevent your heart from being broken by a covenant breaker.

Do not be deceived by the dignified appearance of the unbeliever. He may be a school prefect, a class prefect, a minister of state or even the president. The nature of an unsaved person is described in detail for you in Romans 1:29-31. Believe the Bible more than you believe your eyes. The Bible is the Word of God and is profitable for your instruction.

No one teaches a child to be wicked. Wickedness comes naturally to many little children. Why do children lie, cheat and steal without being taught to do so? It is because the unsaved sprit is at work again.

When I was in secondary school, I couldn't understand the manifestation of wickedness in some of the students. They devised all sorts of unbelievable punishments. When I was in form one, I experienced torture at the hands of senior students. These senior students were not KGB torture specialists. They were just seniors with an unsaved nature.

They could mash chloroquine tablets (a bitter anti-malarial drug) in gari (ground cassava) and give it to people to eat. They had punishments called "tower of liberty" and "monkey dance" which would make all your muscles go into spasms. I was once forced to do a "monkey dance" until I was virtually paralyzed. I couldn't walk for some hours.

Punishments were devised in which you would be sent to collect twenty buckets of manure from a farm two kilometers away. After doing this twenty times, you would have walked eighty kilometers with a heavy load.

Where did all these ideas come from? They originate from the depraved and wicked heart of the unsaved man. I ask myself, "If such people were to come into political power what would they do to their enemies?"

All over the world, the depraved and perverted nature of the human race is manifest. When I hear of the atrocities committed during wars I wonder, "What has come of the human race?" Wickedness abounds in the heart of man because the heart of the unsaved man is dead and desperately wicked. This is not something that affects White people or Black people; it is the nature of all mankind.

During the Liberian Civil War we heard of people being fed to the lions. One Liberian refugee told me how the rebel soldiers would throw children into a well. When the well was full of children they would pour kerosene on top of the screaming children and light a fire. These are real things that actually happened!

Why are human beings so wicked and evil at heart? Why is it that when the opportunity presents itself we see incredible acts of savagery?

A Lebanese man described something that he experienced during the war in Lebanon. He said, "One group would capture some prisoners that belonged to another faction. Then they would amputate the legs and arms of the captives and put the trunk (head, chest and abdomen, without legs and arms) of the people in a car and dispatch them to their homes." He told me how a friend's brother's arms and legs were amputated and how terrible an experience it was.

He continued, "The limbless man was in such a pitiful condition that my friend had to shoot his own brother to end the torture."

These acts of barbarism are manifestations of a depraved and reprobate human race. Why is the world filled with so much evil? Why do millions of people commit fornication and adultery on a daily basis? Why does stealing, killing and injustice abound everywhere? Where is this world of over five billion greedy, corrupt, degenerate and selfish people going?

God has given up the human race to its perverted way of life. It is these unsaved and degenerate people that Jesus came to the earth to save. This is why Jesus said a man had to be born-again. Another term for being born-again is regeneration. When you are born-again, your essential nature is changed. That is why the Bible calls you a new creature. God has to make a new creation out of the old corrupt man.

When a man dies, there is no way you can keep his body at home. No matter how much you love your brother, when the condition called death lays its icy hands on him you have to part company with him. The dead person must go to the mortuary and then the grave. Husbands and wives who love each other have to part when death comes to lay hold on one of them. Why is this? The body of your loved one is dead. It begins to decay and degenerate.

Do you remember what God told Adam and Eve? He said that, "In the day that you eat this fruit you will die." When Adam and Eve sinned, they died. The condition of spiritual death entered their spirits and there was no way God could fellowship with them any more. He had to drag them out of the garden and separate them from Himself. The whole human race is separate from God. Salvation breaks the wall that separates mankind from God.

...and hath broken down the middle wall of partition between us... that he might reconcile both unto God...
Ephesians 2:14

Before a man is born-again, he is estranged from God. His nature is essentially evil. He may look good on the outside, but essentially, he has a corrupt and wicked nature. That is why democracy and the rule of law are important. When one man with such a nature has unlimited power, he does many evil things.

In every nation where there has been a military dictator, inconceivable atrocities have taken place. People are arrested and disappear into "thin air", whilst hard-earned properties are arbitrarily confiscated. Stories of torture, brutality and murder abound. Viciousness in secret and in the open, has always been the order of the day with tyrants.

A tyrant is simply an unsaved man who has unlimited power. That is why many governments have three independent arms: the executive, the legislature and the judiciary. There needs to be a separation of powers because of the wickedness of mankind.

As Lord Acton (1834-1902) said in a letter to Bishop Mandell Creighton, "Power tends to corrupt and absolute power corrupts absolutely."

The difference between Christianity and every other religion is simple. Christianity claims to change the essentially wicked nature of a man. Jesus makes you a new creation. You become a brand new creature with a brand new heart. In the Old Testament, the prophets predicted that the day would come when God would take out the stony heart and replace it with a heart of flesh.

A new heart also I will give you, and a new spirit will I put within you: and I will take away the stony heart out of your flesh, and I will give you an HEART OF FLESH.

Ezekiel 36:26

When a man is in Christ he is a new person. He is regenerated. He is born again. When we speak of being born-again, it does not mean going into your mother's womb again. It is your spirit, the inner nature that is born again.

...that which is born of the Spirit is spirit

John 3:6

If you take a pig and you wash him, bathe him and dress him up in a wedding suit, all you have is a dressed up pig. This same pig will return to the filth which he is used to because that is his essential nature. Obeying a set of rules does not change your heart. Coming to Christ and being born-again is what affords every man the opportunity to have a new heart.

I believe with all my heart that it is only a change in the unsaved nature of a man that can bring about a change in this world. New Year's resolutions and obeying rules do not change anything because the spirit of the unsaved man is dead and desperately wicked. No one toys with a dead thing. Dead things must be separated from living things. The only hope for the dead and wicked human spirit is the miracle of rebirth in Jesus Christ.

3. The spirit of a saved man is righteous and truly holy.

When a man is born-again the spirit within is changed. We have learned earlier that the unsaved spirit is desperately wicked and corrupt. What about the new creation? The new creation is righteous and truly holy!

And that ye put on the new man, which after God is created in RIGHTEOUSNESS AND TRUE HOLINESS.

Ephesians 4:24

This Scripture makes us know that we are actually righteous when we are born-again. What God is telling us is that we must put on (act like) the new spirit which is created in righteousness and true holiness. Many times we come to God and say things that are not true. In an attempt to sound humble, we tell the Lord that we are sinners and we are not worthy to approach His throne. But that is an insult to the new creation. It is time for you to acknowledge what God has done to your heart. The Bible says we are the righteousness of God in Christ Jesus.

For he hath made him to be sin for us, who knew no sin; that we might be made the righteousness of God in him.

2 Corinthians 5:21

If we are the righteousness of God, that means that we cannot be more righteous than we are today. The righteousness of God is the highest form of purity and "sinless-ness". God is describing the status of your new spirit.

Somebody once said, "I don't feel any different now that I'm born-again!" This is not about feelings but about realities that have taken place. Can you feel your liver? Or your small intestines? Obviously not! But they exist within you!

If surgery was performed and your appendix was taken out, the doctors would inform you that they have removed a part of your intestine but you cannot feel it. You are supposed to accept the fact of what has taken place in your abdomen during the surgery. Being born again is a spiritual operation in which God recreates your spirit. He takes out the old hardened and depraved heart and puts in a new and righteous spirit.

The Bible teaches us to acknowledge the good things that are in us because we are Christians. We are not supposed to go around saying negative things about ourselves. If you say, "I am a bad person," you are hurting yourself. If you say, "I'm stupid!" or "I am a sinner" you are saying something that is contrary to the Word of God. It is time to acknowledge good things about yourself.

...by the acknowledging of every good thing which is in you in Christ Jesus.

Philemon 6

Acknowledging good things will make your faith come alive. Say to yourself, "I am the righteousness of God", "I'm a new person!", "I can make it!", "I am holy". These confessions will take you out of sin and into a life of practical holiness. There is always something on the inside that must work on the outside. Righteousness on the inside is working on the outside.

Any born-again Christian who lives in sin, is living contrary to his new nature. If you continue in sin it is by choice because the power of sin is broken and God has given you a new nature. When you are a new creature it is no longer natural to do evil. It is against your very nature as a new creation.

Before you get born again there are evil things you do without even noticing. After you're saved, something within you tells you, "This is wrong! Don't do it!" That is the new man crying from within. The Bible says, "Put on the new man." Act like a new person because you are new.

I became a medical doctor on the 10th of March 1989. On the 11th of March I didn't feel any different; in fact, I still felt like a student. I had to tell myself, "Hey, you are now a doctor. Act like one. Stop acting like a student and act like who you really are." This is what God is saying to His "new creation" children, "You are new, righteous and truly holy. Act like it and walk in the newness of life."

Remember this, righteousness is not a feeling. You do not work to gain righteousness. It is impossible to attain God's standards by your own efforts. Today, if you are born-again, you have been instantaneously transformed into a righteous new man. You cannot be more righteous than the righteousness of God.

You can only increase your faith in your inherited righteousness. You can only practise more and more of your true nature. When you are conscious of your righteousness in Christ, you will become as bold as a lion.

The wicked flee when no man pursueth: but the RIGHTEOUS ARE BOLD AS A LION.

Proverbs 28:1

Through righteousness you will rule and dominate in this life. I see you dominating the enemy through righteousness! I see you overcoming your adversities through the gift of righteousness in Christ Jesus! Stand up now and become a world overcomer!

You are no longer under condemnation.

> **...much more they which receive abundance of grace and the GIFT OF RIGHTEOUSNESS SHALL REIGN in life...**
>
> **Romans 5:17**

4. **After you are born-again, your spirit is a new born baby and it must grow.**

When you get saved, something great has happened. There is no doubt about this. However, we must understand exactly what has happened. When somebody is born into this world, he starts life as a baby. It is important that he matures into an adult.

> **As newborn babes, desire the sincere milk of the word, THAT YE MAY GROW thereby:**
>
> **1 Peter 2:2**

There are times when people have the wrong impression about Christianity. The evangelist preaches and says, "Tonight is your night! Your life will never be the same again after today." He goes on to add, "After tonight, every yoke shall be broken in your life." He declares, "All you who are heavy laden must come to Jesus and He will give you rest." This may give the impression that you instantaneously become a mature Christian.

But that is not the case at all! Being born again is just the beginning of a long process. Being born again is like being born into this world. You must go through three important stages of development. Every Christian goes through these three stages whether he knows it or not! The baby stage, the childhood stage and then the mature adult.

The Spiritual Baby

Let's talk about the baby stage. When a Christian is at the baby stage of his development he has all the characteristics of a natural baby. All babies cry a lot. If you want to know if there is a baby in the house, just stand outside the gate and sooner or later you will hear one crying.

A spiritual baby is easily offended. Anyone who is easily offended is an immature spiritual baby. Little things offend him and he is always upset about one thing or the other. All churches have a lot of babies who are easily offended. But life is full of offenses and you must grow up so that you are not easily offended.

Baby Christians, just like natural babies are unable to help or control themselves. A baby defecates anytime, anywhere and in front of anyone. There are no controls whatsoever. A spiritual baby is unable to control his fleshly appetites. He continues to live in sin. He lives according to the dictates of his flesh and does whatever he feels like doing. As you mature you still have certain feelings but you don't yield to them unless it is appropriate. If you are living on drugs, pornography, immorality and have no control over your flesh, then you are a spiritual baby.

The Childhood Stage

That we be henceforth NO MORE CHILDREN, TOSSED TO AND FRO, and carried about...
                                                                    Ephesians 4:14

There are some important childhood characteristics you must know. A child is unsteady and unstable. It is difficult to hold the attention of a child for more than a few minutes. The attention span of a child is very short. Because of this they are unstable and unreliable. Any Christian who is carried about by every new man of God is a child. If you move around from church to church every few months you are an immature child.

Pastors cannot keep the attention of childlike Christians for more than a few months or years. A man who constantly changes his mind about who he wants to marry is a child at heart. He is unsteady, tossed to and fro by every wind of doctrine and prophecy. Any Christian who can be made to leave his church because of a prophecy delivered to him by the "prophet a la mode" is simply a child who is being tossed to and fro.

There are many childlike Christians in the Church today. Nothing satisfies them for more than a few minutes. Initially they are excited by the good Word. After this, they feel they need special prayers and anointing. After that, they are convinced that a holy bath is what will solve their problems. Nothing seems to satisfy and they are always sniffing for something new.

They come into the church full of praises for the church and its pastor. After a few months, they have changed their minds.

Another sign of a childlike Christian is that he engages in fruitless playful activity. He does not contribute to the home in any way. A Christian who is in the childhood stage does not contribute to the growth of the church. He witnesses to no one and he invites no one.

He does not support financially and does not pay his tithes. Ask yourself this question, "How much money does your child contribute to the upkeep of your home?" Nothing! Is he a part of your home? Certainly! He just plays and makes the house dirty, but contributes nothing. If you are part of a church but contribute nothing to make the church grow and prosper you are a playful child who is enjoying good sermons free of charge. You are certainly a part of the church but you are a child who contributes nothing!

Spiritual Adulthood

But strong meat belongeth to them that are of FULL AGE...

Hebrews 5:14

When you reach the stage of maturity you begin to love the meat of the Word. Bible study and the teaching of the Word are what enchant you. Because the church is comprised of many babies and children, you will discover that a large number of Christians are not interested in the simple teaching of the Word. They want something dramatic and spectacular. Crowds of people gather when there is a sensational minister in the house. A mature person understands the deep things of the Word of God.

Another important feature of a mature person is that he is skillful in the Word of God.

...everyone that uses milk is UNSKILLFUL IN THE WORD OF RIGHTEOUSNESS: for he is a babe.
Hebrews 5:13

When you become skillful in the Word, you begin to teach and preach. Do not make a mistake, every Christian is supposed to develop until he is able to preach and teach. It is not only pastors who are supposed to preach the Word of God. Preaching and teaching is a stage of your Christian development.

For when for THE TIME YE OUGHT TO BE TEACHERS, ye have need that one teach you...
Hebrews 5:12

There is a time when every Christian must be a teacher of God's Word. Let this be your goal from today.

Decide to be someone who is involved in teaching and preaching the Word of God. Until you preach and teach, you are not mature!

How to Develop Your Spirit

The mind is developed in school and colleges. Thousands of dollars are spent to develop the minds of the human race. That explains why we have taken such strides in science and medicine. A lot of money and time is also used to develop the body. There are "keep fit clubs" and gyms everywhere. Men's bodies are being developed into grotesque muscular giants. But dear friend, you are more than a body. You are more than a mind! You are a spirit living in a body and you have a mind. You must also develop your spirit as well. The question is, "How do you develop your spirit into maturity?"

The first key to developing the human spirit is the Word.

...desire the sincere milk of THE WORD, THAT YE MAY GROW thereby:
1 Peter 2:2

Allow the Word of God to enter your spirit through a daily Quiet Time, Bible study and Bible reading. Every Christian must have a Quiet Time every day. I have a Quiet Time with the Lord every day. I benefit greatly from spending time with the Lord every morning. Many of the revelations that the Lord has given me came to me during my Quiet Time.

Moses went up to the mountain early in the morning to meet with the Lord. He took two tables of stone to write down the revelations that God would give him. You need to have a Moses type of Quiet Time. Spend time early in the morning alone with the Lord.

...Hew thee two tables of stone... And be ready in the morning, and come up in the morning... and present thyself there... and no man shall come up with thee...
Exodus 34:1-3

A Quiet Time of Bible study and prayer is the most consistent way to feed your spirit. Your spirit does not grow unless it is fed on the Word of God.

Another good way of taking in the Word is by listening to messages. The second best way by which I have fed my spirit over the years is through listening to preaching and watching church services.

So then faith cometh by hearing, and hearing by the word of God
Romans 10:17

I listen to preaching all the time and I am blessed. God has given pastors and teachers to perfect the saints. You can receive the Word through these anointed men of God.

Another way that you can develop your spirit is by praying in tongues. Every Christian must develop the art of spending hours praying in the spirit. The Bible says you build up yourself in the faith when you pray in the Holy Ghost. Praying in the Holy Ghost is the same as praying in tongues.

But ye, beloved, **BUILDING UP YOURSELVES** on your most holy faith, praying in the Holy Ghost.

Jude 20

Pray in tongues for an hour everyday. Watch what will happen in your spiritual life over the next three months. The Bible teaches us that you are spiritually charged and built up when you speak in tongues.

He that speaketh in an unknown tongue, edifieth himself...

1 Corinthians 14:4

The Word and prayer will cause you to develop in the spirit and to become a giant for the Lord. Walk in these two keys of spiritual growth and nothing will be held back from you. I see God taking you out of your hiding place! I see Him placing you before kings and prominent men as you develop your spirit!

5. **After you are saved your mind is still the same; it must be renewed.**

   And be not conformed to this world: but be ye transformed by the RENEWING OF YOUR MIND that ye may prove what is that good, and acceptable, and perfect, will of God

   Romans 12:2

When you are born again, it is the spirit that is changed. God gives you a new heart and not a new mind. It is therefore the duty of every Christian to renew his mind. If you do not renew your mind, you will be a person with a new spirit and an old mind. There are many Christians who are genuine new creations but still have an unrenewed mind.

If you belong to a good church which constantly preaches and teaches the Word of God, your mind will be renewed. There are many people who think that they know all there is to know in the Word of God. No one knows everything!

Every Christian must decide to be a constant learner of the Word of God. He must never stop learning. You will always discover things that you do not know. Years ago I heard a pastor giving a testimony of his life. He spoke about how he got born again. Before he was saved he was a pornographer by profession. That means he was someone who acted in pornographic films and posed for pornographic photographs. Sex was his work and he didn't see anything wrong with it.

He told us one day, "When I got born again I continued to live in fornication."

"I slept with girl after girl and I never thought twice about it. It never occurred to me that there was anything wrong with sleeping with someone you're not married to."

He continued, "I thought I was being a loving person to many girls. After all, love is a commandment from God." One night he was in bed with one of the numerous girls. Suddenly a huge black figure appeared at the foot of his bed and he woke up in great fright.

He was terrified and thought to himself, "Something is not right!"

The next day he decided to read the Bible and discovered where the Word of God says fornication is wrong. Believe it or not, this man was born again but because of his background, he did not even know that fornication was sin.

It could be that because of your background you are not even aware that certain things are sin. I know many Christians who are prejudiced or racist. There are even pastors who are racist in their thoughts and decisions. Without even realizing it, we carry on doing wrong things although we are genuinely born again in our hearts. That is why we need the Word of God to renew our minds.

...be ye transformed by the RENEWING OF YOUR MIND...

Romans 12:2

It is actually the renewing of our minds that brings about a visible transformation.

45

When I became a Christian, I thought God wanted us to be poor. Somehow, my background taught me that poverty was more righteous than prosperity. If you read the Bible your mind will be renewed and your attitude will change. Transformation comes when the mind is renewed. The real change we see in Christians comes through a renewal of the mind through the Word of God.

See your mind as a computer which has to be programmed. Whatever you feed into the mind is what will come out.

There are many Christians who do not pay tithes simply because their minds are polluted with wrong ideas. Some people think there is no need to do any such thing. Some think the pastors are just using the money for their extravagant lifestyle.

However, every Christian who has his mind renewed will find himself being transformed in the area of his finances.

Even though you are born again your mind is still the same. It must be renewed with the Word of God. It must be re-programed. It is a computer which must be re-programed.

6. **After you are saved your body is still the same, and you must keep it under control.**

When you get saved, you must know that your body is the same old body. When you are a new creation you do not change physically! If you were tall and skinny before salvation, you will still be tall and skinny after salvation. If you had long hair before you got born again, you'll still have long hair after salvation. What does this mean? Does it mean that nothing has happened to you? Not at all!

Your body is the same even though you are born again. You must understand this all important fact.

When people give their lives to Christ they believe that everything is going to be different just as the preacher said. However, when they get home they begin to feel the old feelings they felt before salvation. They experience lusts and fears within their bodies.

Because they are newly born again the devil lies to them and tells them, "You are not a real Christian." "You cannot be born-again!"

Satan continues to harass them and say, "If you were really born again, such thoughts and feelings would never come to you."

The devil tells them, "None of the Christians sitting in this church have the kind of thoughts you have."

But that is a lie! Everyone who is born again still has the flesh to contend with. Paul was worried about his flesh. He knew that his body was still the same. He knew that his flesh could disgrace him one day so he said, "I keep my flesh under control."

I KEEP MY BODY UNDER [control] and bring it under subjection lest by any means when I preach to others I myself should be a castaway.

1 Corinthians 9:27

Paul is the one who had a personal revelation of Jesus Christ! Paul wrote half of the New Testament! Paul had so many visions and revelations of Jesus Christ! Very few people have had such spiritual experiences. Paul was one of the greatest apostles with signs and wonders following him. He raised the dead and the bites of snakes had no effect on him!

Yet, this great man was worried about his flesh. He felt his flesh could disgrace him at any time. That is why he kept his flesh under constant control. Notice what he said in the book of Romans. He declared that there was nothing good in his flesh. Even though he was born again, his flesh (body) was still the same.

For I know that in me (that is, in my flesh,) dwelleth no good thing...

Romans 7:18

No matter who you are, you still have a body to keep under control. Have you ever seen a spirit smoking or drinking alcohol?

47

Certainly not! Spirits don't smoke! It is the flesh that drinks and smokes! Have you ever seen a spirit committing fornication? Surely not! It is the flesh that does all these evil things! That is why the Bible teaches us to present our bodies as a living sacrifice.

The works of the flesh are listed in Galatians chapter five.

Now the works of the flesh are manifest, which are these; Adultery, fornication, uncleanness, lasciviousness, Idolatry, witchcraft, hatred, variance, emulations, wrath, strife, seditions, heresies, Envyings, murders, drunkenness, revellings, and such like: of the which I tell you before, as I have
Galatians 5:19-21

These works are not the works of Satan or evil spirits. They are the works of the flesh. Look at the list again. Adultery, fornication, witchcraft, hatred, wrath, murder, drunkenness, envyings and the list goes on.

Mind you, these are not the works of "unbelievers' flesh". These are the works of the flesh. Do you have flesh? Of course you do! You have a body and so do I. That means that both you and I are capable of this list of horrible deeds! The flesh is a real burden that we are saddled with through this life.

One day when Jesus comes we shall be changed. Our bodies shall be transformed into immortal and incorruptible bodies. We will no longer be capable of sin.

...We shall not all sleep, but we shall all be changed... for the trumpet shall sound, and the dead shall be raised incorruptible and we shall be changed. For this corruptible shall put on incorruption and this mortal must put on immortality.
1 Corinthians 15:51-53

One day, I went to visit a friend of mine. He was a hardened sinner who was not interested in being born again. I sat with him in his bedroom and we chatted for many hours. At a point, the

Holy Spirit made a way for me to witness to him about Christ. That was his day of salvation. For the first time, he listened to me as I preached to him. When I finished, he asked me, "What must I do?"

I said, "Let us pray and I will lead you to the Lord."

After I led him in the sinner's prayer, he looked at me and said, "Dag, thank you very much. I feel I am a changed person."

Then I thought, "If I have been able to lead my friend to the Lord, why don't I lead him to receive the baptism of the Holy Spirit? I decided to do just that. I laid hands on him and to my surprise he received the Holy Spirit and began to speak in tongues fluently. Suddenly something else happened. When I touched him, he was "slain in the Spirit" and fell on his bed.

He continued to bubble in tongues for some time. After about an hour I decided to leave and come back to see him later.

About five hours later I returned to his house to visit him. When I got to the gate his sister told me that she didn't think he was home. But I went to his apartment anyway. When I got there, something told me to pause at the door before going in. I stood at the door and what did I hear? My new convert was having sex in the bedroom with a girlfriend. I was aghast!

Less than five hours ago this man had received Christ and was gloriously filled with the Holy Spirit. I personally ministered to him and saw him speaking in tongues and being "slain in the Spirit". How could he return so quickly into fornication? I asked myself, "Was this man really born again?" Does being born again have any effect on a person? The answer is, "Yes, it does!"

If anyone was ever born again and filled with the Holy Spirit, this friend of mine was. The reality was that the body was still the same and was capable of committing all the sins of the flesh. Never forget this! Even though you are born again, your flesh is still the same, you must keep it under control otherwise it will lead you into sin.

Control Your Flesh

There are some practical ways by which you can keep your body under control. Firstly, be aware of the potential evil that is in your flesh. Spend time fasting on a regular weekly basis. Do not give opportunities to your flesh.

...only use not liberty for an occasion to the flesh...
Galatians 5:13

The reason why boarding schools have separate houses for boys and girls is because the school authorities do not want to give occasion and opportunity to the flesh. If you expose yourself to certain things, you will fall.

If I expose myself to certain things, I will fall. What we need is wisdom to help us to control our flesh till we die.

7. **After you are born again, your mind is still open to all kinds of thoughts, you must learn to think on the right things.**

You may be a born-again Christian. You may keep your body under subjection. You may renew your mind on the Word of God regularly. But this does not close your mind to the attacks of the devil. Your mind is still open to all kinds of thoughts from the devil.

When Satan attacked Jesus, he attacked His mind. The devil appealed to His mind. The devil will always appeal to your mind. The Bible teaches us that we must cast down imaginations.

Casting down imaginations, and every high thing that exalteth itself against the knowledge of God, and bringing into captivity every thought to the obedience of Christ
2 Corinthians 10:5

Remember this truth: your mind is the battleground. Satan's most powerful tool is suggestion. Jesus was tempted through the avenue of His thoughts. The fact that you are a Christian does not mean that you will only have good thoughts. A thought is like a bird that flies over your head. It may land on your head, but it must not be allowed to make a nest on your head.

When ungodly thoughts come to you, resist them immediately. Do not be surprised when outrageous things occur to you. That is the fight of every born-again Christian; to keep your mind pure at all times. Some Christians are plagued with fear and worry. Fear is one of the terrible thoughts of the devil.

Whilst working on the hospital ward as a medical student, I remember seeing many young patients die. I began to think about their plight and a spirit of fear oppressed me. The thoughts were so overwhelming that I had to sleep in order to forget what I was thinking about. Many times I saw myself sick and dying of the same disease. I imagined my funeral and I imagined what I would look like in the coffin.

I thought about all those who would attend my funeral and I worked out every detail in my mind. I was truly oppressed by the evil thoughts of fear that ravaged my mind.

Dear friend, fear is an oppressive spirit that works through the mind. Whether it is worry, fear, or lust, you must learn to cast down imaginations. You must learn to capture your thoughts and make them obedient to the Word of God. You must resist the devil.

...and bringing into captivity every thought to the obedience of Christ

2 Corinthians 10:5

You must resist the devil in your life. When the Word of God says you must resist the devil, it means that you must resist thoughts and suggestions that come from the pit of Hell.

The Bible tells us exactly what to think about. It tells us to think of things that are pure, holy and peaceful.

Finally, brethren, whatsoever things are true, whatsoever things are honest, whatsoever things are

just, whatsoever things are pure, whatsoever things are lovely, whatsoever things are of good report; if there be any virtue, and if there be any praise, think on these things.

Philippians 4:8

Control Your Thoughts

One of the best ways to control your thoughts is to listen to preaching. Christian music and videos are good tools to help in controlling your thoughts. Do not give place to the devil! You give place to the devil when you allow evil thoughts to settle in your mind. They will oppress and obsess you until you become possessed.

You must grow in your understanding about salvation through these seven great principles. In all your getting get understanding. Wisdom is the principal thing. The people who understand what is happening are the people who will experience God's victory.

CHAPTER 4

What Will Happen to You When You Die?

There was a certain rich man, which was clothed in purple and fine linen, and fared sumptuously every day:
And there was a certain beggar named Lazarus, which was laid at his gate, full of sores, and desiring to be fed with the crumbs which fell from the rich man's table: moreover the dogs came and licked his sores.
And it came to pass, that the beggar died, and was carried by the angels into Abraham's bosom: the rich man also died, and was buried; and in hell he lift up his eyes, being in torments, and seeth Abraham afar off, and Lazarus in his bosom. And he cried and said, Father Abraham, have mercy on me, and send Lazarus, that he may dip the tip of his finger in water, and cool my tongue; for I am tormented in this flame.
But Abraham said, Son, remember that thou in thy lifetime receivedst thy good things, and likewise Lazarus evil things: but now he is comforted, and thou art tormented.
And beside all this, between us and you there is a great gulf fixed: so that they which would pass from hence to you cannot; neither can they pass to us, that would come from thence. Then he said, I pray thee

therefore, father, that thou wouldest send him to my father's house: For I have five brethren; that he may testify unto them, lest they also come into this place of torment.

Abraham saith unto him, They have Moses and the prophets; let them hear them. And he said, Nay, father Abraham: but if one went unto them from the dead, they will repent. And he said unto him, If they hear not Moses and the prophets, neither will they be persuaded, though one rose from the dead.

Luke 16:19-31

One of the most important questions to ask yourself is: "What will happen to me when I die?" This is a question that cannot be easily answered by university lecturers or school teachers. There are no textbooks that fearlessly and adequately answer the question of what happens to a man when he dies. The Bible is the only book that confidently answers this controversial and difficult question.

Both the rich and the poor will die. The Bible declares that after death there will be judgement. Rich men are likely to live longer than the poor. However, both of them will eventually die. Death is the leveller that will level out things for both the rich and the poor.

Fifteen Things That Will Happen When You Die

1. **When you die you will either go to Heaven or Hell.** The rich man went to Hell and Lazarus went to Heaven. You will not just stop existing. You are not just converted into a piece of meat. You will head for a permanent destination away from this earth – Heaven or Hell.

    And it came to pass, that the beggar died, and was carried by the angels into Abraham's bosom: the rich man also died, and was buried; And in hell he lifted up his eyes, being in torments, and seeth Abraham afar off, and Lazarus in his bosom.

    Luke 16:22-23

2. **If you go to Heaven when you die, angels will come to escort and carry you away from this earth into the presence of God.** This is what happened to Lazarus and I expect nothing less than a similar angelic escort for all of us who know the Lord.

    And it came to pass, that the beggar died, and was carried by the angels into Abraham's bosom:

    Luke 16:22

3. **If you go to Hell when you die you will be met on arrival by evil spirits and other dead people.** This will be one of the most unpleasant experiences of your life: Your arrival into the permanent abode of darkness, demons and wicked fallen beings.

Hell from BENEATH is moved for thee to meet thee at thy coming: it stirreth up the dead for thee, even all the chief ones of the earth; it hath raised up from their thrones all the kings of the nations.

Isaiah 14:9

4. **When you die you will go downward if you are going to Hell. Hell is below.** Hell is beneath us. The Scripture says, "Hell from beneath is moved for thee..." That is why the rich man had to lift up his eyes to see Abraham afar off. The rich man was down below; that was why he had to lift up his eyes to see Lazarus.

And it came to pass, that the beggar died, and was carried by the angels into Abraham's bosom: the rich man also died, and was buried; And in hell he LIFT UP his eyes, being in torments, and seeth Abraham afar off, and Lazarus in his bosom.

Luke 16:22-23

5. **When you die you will discover that you have a spiritual body of a man which the Bible refers to as the inward man.** When Jesus told the story of Lazarus, he referred to different body parts such as the tongue, the finger and the eyes. It is evident that there is another man within. This inward man will live forever; either in Heaven or in Hell.

And he cried and said, Father Abraham, have mercy on me, and send Lazarus, that he may dip the tip of his finger in water, and cool my tongue; for I am tormented in this flame

Luke 16:24

6. **If you go to Hell when you die you will find yourself in a prison where there is ENDLESS unimaginable distress and torment with intolerable agony.** The endlessness of the agonies of Hell are depicted by the worm that does not die and the fire that is not quenched.

And if thy hand offend thee, cut it off: it is better for thee to enter into life maimed, than having two hands to go into hell, into the fire that never shall be quenched: Where their worm DIETH NOT, and the fire is not quenched.

Mark 9:43-44

7. **If you go to Hell when you die you will discover a place where people scream and cry for a drop of water. Nobody asks for a bottle of water in Hell.** No one asks whether the water is cold or not. No one asks for ice. No one even asks for a small glass of water. Just a drop of water would make all the difference in Hell. I honestly cannot imagine what kind of place Hell is.

And he cried and said, Father Abraham, have mercy on me, and send Lazarus, that he may dip the tip of his finger in water, and cool my tongue; for I am tormented in this flame.

Luke 16:24

8. **If you go to Hell when you die you will discover a place of unbelievable and indescribable anguish and torment.**

And he cried and said, Father Abraham, have mercy on me, and send Lazarus, that he may dip the tip of his finger in water, and cool my tongue; for I am tormented in this flame

Luke 16:24

9. **When you die you will discover that many people who received good things on earth will receive evil things in Hell and many people who received evil things on earth will receive good things in Heaven.** Many of those who

suffered on earth will receive good things and many of those who received evil things on earth will receive good things in Heaven.

But Abraham said, Son, remember that thou in thy lifetime receivedst thy good things, and likewise Lazarus evil things: but now he is comforted, and thou art tormented.

Luke 16:25

10. **When you die you will discover that the first shall be last and the last shall be first.** In Heaven, the poor man was in a better place than the rich man. There was a complete reversal of status. The rich man was down, down, down. The rich man was powerless. The rich man was suffering. The rich man needed water. The rich man needed help. The rich man was crying out of his pain and his need.

Do you remember that all these things were happening to the poor man on earth? On earth, the poor man was down, down, down needing help, and water. On earth, the poor man was powerless as he suffered and cried out in pain from his sores.

The words of Jesus will come to pass with such frightening accuracy making no sense of all the things we valued whilst on earth.

But Abraham said, Son, remember that thou in thy lifetime receivedst thy good things, and likewise Lazarus evil things: but now he is comforted, and thou art tormented.

Luke 16:25

11. **When you die your circumstances will change radically. If you were a rich man who used to send people on errands, you will no longer be able to do that.** In the story that Jesus told, the rich man tried to send the poor man Lazarus on an errand, but he was blocked. Things had changed and rich men were no longer allowed to do their own thing. What a drastic change of circumstances.

And he cried and said, Father Abraham, have mercy on me, and SEND LAZARUS, that he may dip the tip of his finger in water, and cool my tongue; for I am tormented in this flame.

Luke 16:24

12. **When you die you will remember everything that happened on earth.** You will remember the opportunities you had. You will remember the messages you heard. You will remember your sins, and you will remember the altar calls you did not respond to. You will wish you had lived your life with the reality of Heaven and Hell always on your heart.

But Abraham said, Son, remember that thou in thy lifetime receivedst thy good things, and likewise Lazarus evil things: but now he is comforted, and thou art tormented.

Luke 16:25

13. **When you die you will discover that there is a big gap between Heaven and Hell.** People cannot cross over from Hell to Heaven no matter who they are and no matter how much money they had on earth.

If you want to cross you must cross now because you cannot transfer when you die. This reality will be difficult for people who are used to using their connections and friends in high places to get what they want. There will be no one in any high place to contact.

One of my children was privileged to attend a prestigious school in Ghana. This school originally had the capacity for only two hundred and fifty children but it had been expanded to house one thousand, five hundred children. After the school had admitted the new entrants who really qualified, other students were mysteriously added to the school population every day. My child told me how a new student arrived in the school every single day. Everyone in the school knew that these were children who were connected to the rich and powerful in the Ghanaian society.

People who live in the African world are so used to getting things done through "connections" – whom you know. The reality of Heaven and Hell will be a great shock to this African culture. People will not be transferred from Hell to Heaven every week because of whom they know. Salvation will be through the blood of Jesus and not through "whom you know".

And beside all this, between us and you there is a great gulf fixed: so that they which would pass from hence to you cannot; neither can they pass to us, that would come from thence.

Luke 16:26

14. **When you die you will discover the importance of evangelists who go all over the world preaching the gospel.** You will appreciate the value of gospel crusades, evangelistic breakfast meetings, gospel concerts, Christian literature, tracts and Christian television outreach programmes.

You will wish there had been more of these easily-criticized preachers. You will wish to swallow any words of criticism you have ever uttered about pastors and evangelists.

Then he said, I pray thee therefore, father, that thou wouldest send him to my father's house:

For I have five brethren; that he may testify unto them, lest they also come into this place of torment.

Abraham saith unto him, They have Moses and the prophets; let them hear them. And he said, Nay, father Abraham: but if one went unto them from the dead, they will repent.

Luke 16:27-30

15. When you die you will only care about people not going to Hell. You will not care about your money or your property. Most ministers of the gospel do not have the drive for soul winning that the rich man had when he was in Hell.

If you are born again when you die you will be glad that Jesus Christ came to die on the cross to shed His blood for you. You will be glad that God so loved the world that He gave His only begotten son that whosoever believes in Him should not perish but have everlasting life.

Then he said, I pray thee therefore, father, that thou wouldest send him to my father's house: For I have five brethren; that he may testify unto them, lest they also come into this place of torment.

Luke 16:27-28

CHAPTER 5

What Kind of People Will Be in Hell?

Who's who in any community speaks of the outstanding or influential persons in that community, profession or group. We now want to know who and who will be the outstanding personalities in the community of outer darkness. In other words, who exactly is going to be in Hell?

Who is Who in Hell?

1. **Many rich people will be in Hell.**

   ...THE RICH MAN ALSO DIED, and was buried; AND IN HELL HE LIFT UP HIS EYES, being in torments, and seeth Abraham afar off, and Lazarus in his bosom.

   Luke 16:22-23

   Christ died to save you from perishing in Hell. A place is made intolerable by the type of people that are there. The intolerable nature of Hell is created by the presence of the most evil men who ever lived as well as the presence of evil spirits, the false prophet, the dragon and fallen angels.

The Fake Politician

I remember a rich politician of a certain country who went to jail for various crimes. When he entered the prison he was so frightened by the kind of people that were there that he feigned sickness immediately and asked to be admitted in the hospital.

In that country, if you had enough money you could pay to be in a hospital that was not in the prison. This rich man continued to pay thousands of dollars so that he could stay out of the frightening prison. In the end, his money ran out and he had to go back to face the people in prison. Hopefully, this rich man would serve his sentence and come out of prison. But there is a prison which you can never climb out of. That is the fate of many rich men who descend into Hell with no chance of parole. They are shocked to find that they have descended into a horrible pit, wherein dwell the most evil men that ever lived! The Bible tells us that the rich man went to Hell.

2. **Wicked people will be in Hell.**

THE WICKED SHALL BE TURNED INTO HELL, and all the nations that forget God.

Psalms 9:17

The Frightened Prisoner

One day, after preaching a man walked up to me and introduced himself as an ex-convict. He described how he had been in prison for the past fifteen years. As he talked with me, I realised how nervous and edgy he was, casting furtive glances across his shoulder every few seconds.

At a point, I asked him what was wrong. He apologised for his unusually restless and jumpy attitude. He explained, "I am always scared because I think somebody is going to attack me from behind. I was twenty years old when I went to prison and I am now thirty-five years old.

He went on, "In jail there were so many murderers and rapists. You were always in danger of being attacked from behind. That is why I am so nervous."

63

That is what makes prison frightening. I began to understand what it means to be in a prison. I understood even more what it meant to go to Hell and be caged in with frightening characters like witches, wizards and murderers. Hell is a place to avoid at all costs.

3. People who forget God and those who do not acknowledge God will be in Hell.

The wicked shall be turned into hell, AND ALL THE NATIONS THAT FORGET GOD.

Psalms 9:17

There are many people who have put God out of their lives and their careers. They have forgotten that there is a God somewhere. Many people in Europe believe that there is no God. They do not believe in God, they do not pray to God and they do not go to church any more. They may do good deeds and finance huge humanitarian programmes but they will be turned into Hell because they forgot that there is a God. It is a fool who says in his heart that there is no God.

You will notice how some politicians do not acknowledge God when they win elections. They forget about God and do not acknowledge Him. They may acknowledge their wives, their children and their dogs but forget to acknowledge God. This is very dangerous because they that forget God will be turned to Hell.

The fool hath said in his heart, There is no God. They are corrupt, they have done abominable works, there is none that doeth good.

Psalms 14:1

And just as they DID NOT SEE FIT TO ACKNOWLEDGE GOD ANY LONGER, God gave them over to a depraved mind, to do those things which are not proper, being filled with all unrighteousness, wickedness, greed, evil; full of envy, murder, strife, deceit, malice; they are gossips, slanderers, haters of God, insolent, arrogant, boastful, inventors of evil, disobedient to parents, without understanding, untrustworthy, unloving, unmerciful; and, although they know the ordinance of God, that THOSE WHO PRACTICE SUCH THINGS ARE WORTHY OF DEATH, they not only do the same, but also give hearty approval to those who practice them.

Romans 1:28-32, (NASB)

4. The pompous, the mighty and proud, the chief ones of the earth will be in Hell.

HELL FROM BENEATH IS MOVED FOR THEE TO MEET THEE at thy coming: it stirreth up the dead for thee, even all THE CHIEF ONES OF THE EARTH; it hath raised up from their thrones all the kings of the nations.

All they shall speak and say unto thee, Art thou also become weak as we? art thou become like unto us?

THY POMP IS BROUGHT DOWN to the grave, and the noise of thy viols: the worm is spread under thee, and the worms cover thee.

Isaiah 14:9-11

The big shots of the earth will be crowding themselves into the dark spaces of Hell. The Bible speaks of the chief ones of the earth. The Bible describes how their ostentation and showiness will be brought down to nothing. Unfortunately, this will be the portion of the glamorous and flamboyant peoples of the earth.

5. The beast will be in Hell.

And THE BEAST was taken, and with him the false prophet that wrought miracles before him, with which he deceived them that had received the mark of the beast, and them that worshipped his image. These both were CAST ALIVE INTO A LAKE OF FIRE burning with brimstone.

Revelation 19:20

The beast, who is the Antichrist and the most evil man that ever lived will also be among the community in Hell. He will have his place there forever and all those who go to Hell will have to contend with him.

6. The false prophet will be in Hell.

And the beast was taken, and with him THE FALSE PROPHET that wrought miracles before him, with which he deceived them that had received the mark of the beast, and them that worshipped his image. These both were CAST ALIVE INTO A LAKE OF FIRE burning with brimstone.

Revelation 19:20

The false prophet who can be likened to the spiritual wizard of the Antichrist will also be in Hell. This evil man whose spiritual charms, enchantments and spells were used to empower the Antichrist will also be in Hell.

7. The devil himself will be in Hell.

And the devil that deceived them was cast into the lake of fire and brimstone, where the beast and the false prophet are, and shall be tormented day and night for ever and ever.

Revelation 20:10

Another person who will be among the community in Hell is the devil himself. All those who have been afraid of demons and devils and ghosts will have to deal with the devil himself in the misty darkness of the underworld. The devil himself will be one of the most prominent and important members of the vast community found in Hell.

CHAPTER 6

What Is Happening in Hell?

C hrist died to save us from perishing in the lake of fire. All through the Bible we are told that there is a place called Hell. The lake of fire is the final destination for all who go to Hell.

A Room-Mate in Hell

I once heard a startling story of how the Lord Jesus appeared to an Assemblies of God pastor in a vision and told him, "I want you to become more evangelistic so I am going to take you to Hell so you see how real it is."

This pastor had known the Lord from his youth but when he became a teenager he backslid and forsook God. This backsliding continued until he went to the university, where he re-dedicated his life to the Lord. In fact, he was so zealous that he left college and decided to go into Bible School and into the ministry. It was whilst he was a pastor that the Lord appeared to him one Sunday night to urge him to be more evangelistic.

During the vision the Lord took him to Hell where he saw all the sights and sounds of Hell. He saw the weeping, the gnashing and the wailing of the lost. He said, "If the Lord had not been with me, I would have been really frightened of what I saw in Hell."

Suddenly, they came across someone in Hell whom he recognized. This person was his second year room-mate whilst in college.

He exclaimed, "What are you doing here?"

To his amazement his room-mate said, "I was killed in an automobile accident on Friday."

Remember that this vision took place on Sunday night.

When he came out of the vision, he was so disturbed and wanted to call his mother and find out if she knew anything about his room-mate but it was too late to call. So he called his mother on Monday. After exchanging niceties with her he asked, "Have you heard from so-so and so, my room-mate?"

His mother answered, "I was going to tell you, he was killed in a terrible car accident on Friday."

The pastor could not believe his ears. He was in shock. It was real. He had actually seen his second year room-mate in Hell. He had actually seen the inside of the prison and his own friend and room-mate in it.

Dear friend, Hell is real and the people in Hell know and remember how they died! They know when they died! They have experienced Hell first-hand and found out that the Bible is true! The Bible contains the word of God. The Bible gives the only reliable information we have about Hell.

What the Bible Says about Hell

1. Hell is a vast lake of burning brimstone (sulphur).

And the devil that deceived them was cast into the lake of fire and brimstone (burning sulphur), where the beast and the false prophet are, and shall be tormented day and night for ever and ever.

Revelation 20:10

There are many huge lakes of burning sulphur on the earth today. We call them volcanoes and indeed they are a sober reminder and a sober warning of the reality of the eternal lake of fire.

Burning sulphur has an acrid odour that is found in volcanoes. It is a marvel that modern sceptics cannot imagine lakes that are continually on fire. But volcanoes are burning lakes of fire found in different mountains all over the earth.

Many of these volcanoes have been simmering for hundreds of years and no one has asked how the liquid fire in these vast lakes is kept ablaze.

2. Hell is a place of sorrows.

The sorrows of hell compassed me about; the snares of death prevented me;

2 Samuel 22:6

There are so many well-known sorrows on this earth. However the Bible warns of the sorrows of Hell. If the sorrows of this earth are difficult to bear how much more terrible will the sorrows of Hell be? Hell is a place to avoid because of the sorrows there.

3. Hell is a place where you never die and where the suffering never ends.

And in those days shall men seek death, and shall not find it; and shall desire to die, and death shall flee from them.

Revelation 9:6

And if thy hand offend thee, cut it off: it is better for thee to enter into life maimed, than having two hands to go into hell, into the fire that never shall be quenched:

69

WHERE THEIR WORM DIETH NOT, AND THE FIRE
IS NOT QUENCHED.

Mark 9:43-44

The Husband Who Thought He Could End It All

The endlessness of Hell is perhaps the most frightening aspect of all. I heard the true story of a Swiss lady who was suffering in the hospital from terminal cancer. Her husband visited her every day and watched his wife suffer and deteriorate. His wife who was constantly writhing in agony desperately wanted to die.

One day, he decided to end it all himself. Since he was a member of the reserve army of Switzerland, he went home, took his gun, went back to the hospital and shot his wife. Then he handed himself over to the police. He could not stand the suffering of his wife any longer and he decided to end it all. This gentleman was happy with the outcome because he knew he had ended his wife's suffering on this earth.

As I thought of this story, I remembered what Jesus had said about a place where the suffering never ends. You will not be able to take a gun and end anything. The worm never dies and the heat is never lowered.

Five Things That Are Happening in Hell

1. **What is happening in Hell? Something so terrible is happening in Hell that it is worth giving up your arms, eyes and legs in order to avoid going there. Hell is so difficult that you cannot even imagine the suffering that is experienced by those over there.**

   And if thy hand offend thee, cut it off: it is better for thee to enter into life maimed, than HAVING TWO HANDS TO GO INTO HELL, into the fire that never shall be quenched: Where their worm dieth not, and the fire is not quenched.

   And if thy foot offend thee, cut it off: it is better for thee to enter halt into life, than having two feet to be cast into hell, into the fire that never shall be quenched:

Where their worm dieth not, and the fire is not quenched.

And if thine eye offend thee, pluck it out: it is better for thee to enter into the kingdom of God with one eye, than having two eyes to be cast into hell fire:

Mark 9:43-47

I know of no place on earth that is worth giving up your arms or your eyes for. Perhaps there is no stronger description to help us comprehend the kind of place that Hell must be. A place so terrible that you would gladly offer your eyes or your arms to escape from!

2. **What is happening in Hell? Millions of people are bound in chains in the vast dark, misty, scary dungeons of the underworld.**

For if God spared not the angels that sinned, but cast them down to hell, and delivered them into CHAINS OF DARKNESS, to be reserved unto judgment

2 Peter 2:4

To be bound for a few hours is a hard enough experience. I cannot fathom what it must be like to be bound forever in chains of darkness.

3. **What is happening in Hell? People are burning alive in the lake of fire. They are not dying and they are not being extinguished. Rather, they are continuing to live in the fire, the heat and the darkness of Hell.**

And the beast was taken, and with him the false prophet that wrought miracles before him, with which he deceived them that had received the mark of the beast, and them that worshipped his image. These both were cast alive into A LAKE OF FIRE burning with brimstone.

Revelation 19:20

You will not drown in the lake. Neither will you be burnt to ashes. You will be alive whilst in this fire. This is not comparable to death by firing squad, drowning, hanging, poisoning or even electrocution. In those cases, death comes after a few minutes.

The horrors of the execution scene will pass away quickly whilst you are transported into another world. However, in this lake of fire, you will be alive whilst you are being burnt and drowned. Meanwhile, you will never fully drown or fully get burnt.

4. **What is happening in Hell? Hell is receiving new admissions everyday but does not seem to be getting full. The lake of fire will never be full because the Bible says Hell is never full.**

Hell and destruction are never full; so the eyes of man are never satisfied.

Prov 27:20

There is space for you in Hell if you stubbornly refuse gospel salvation through Christ.

5. **What is happening in Hell? There are huge expansion projects taking place in Hell. Hell is expanding! Hell is enlarging!**

Therefore HELL HATH ENLARGED HERSELF, and opened her mouth without measure: and their glory, and their multitude, and their pomp, and he that rejoiceth, shall descend into it.

Isaiah 5:14

Because the majority of people are on the broad way, there are endless numbers of people heading towards Hell.

The lake of fire is being expanded because more and more people are rejecting God in their pride. Multitudes await the good news of Jesus Christ in the corners of the earth whilst we celebrate over nothing in our big city churches.

CHAPTER 7

How the Blood of Jesus Can Save You from Hell?

1. The blood of Jesus has the supernatural power to save you from the consequences of your sin.

Forasmuch as ye know that ye were not REDEEMED with corruptible things, as silver and gold, from your vain conversation received by tradition from your fathers; But WITH THE PRECIOUS BLOOD OF CHRIST, as of a lamb without blemish and without spot:

1 Peter 1:18-19

The Search

I once knew somebody who was dying in the hospital and needed blood so that he could be saved. I got involved and went to the blood bank myself. When I entered the bank I saw blood in packets lying all over the place. There was some blood on the table and there was also blood in the fridge. I looked into the fridge myself and saw several shelves laden with blood. But there was a problem. They did not have the right blood for my friend. My friend's blood was a rare type.

73

"Sorry, we don't have the type of blood that you need," they said.

"What do you mean by that? Is this animal blood? Is it the blood of goats or the blood of bulls?"

"We don't have goat blood here!" they exclaimed. "Goat blood does not go with human blood."

Your friend needs a special type of human blood which we do not have.

Then I asked about the blood on the table. They said, "This blood has expired. It cannot be used any more."

"What do you mean by 'expired'?" I asked.

"It is too old," they said. "It has lost its power."

"Wow!"I thought to myself. "Then the blood of Jesus is really powerful, to have lasted for more than two thousand years without losing its power."

That night I realized how true it was that there were different kinds of blood. There were many kinds of blood but none of them was appropriate. That night I realized that all the blood in the bank could not save my friend. It was simply not the right kind of blood. It was either expired blood, or the wrong kind of blood. I began to make calls to other hospitals to see if I could find some appropriate blood for my friend.

You see, dear brother, the blood of bulls and goats could never have the power to save you from your sins. Only the blood of the sinless Lamb of God has the power to wash away sins.

This is why we sing about the blood of Jesus. This is why we sing, "There is power, power, wonder-working power in the blood of the Lamb."

This is why we also sing that the blood will never lose its power. The blood of Jesus will last forever. It is eternal blood and it will always have the power to wash away sins.

The Murderer

One day I visited a high security prison in Africa. I was slated to preach to the inmates on death row that morning. Everybody in the section I went to was condemned to death. I was met at the sectional gate of that prison by a Bible-wielding gentleman who introduced himself as the leader of the fellowship. He looked and sounded like any ordinary pastor you would meet in a church. I asked him who he was.

He said, "I'm the leader of the fellowship in the condemned cells." I was amazed that such a spiritual, Bible-wielding person would be in this place. I gathered courage and asked him, "What did you do that brought you to this prison?"

He smiled sheepishly at me and said, "Oh, murder. Everyone in this section has been convicted of murder."

I was silent for a while and wondered how such a nice person could kill anyone.

Then I asked him, "Who did you kill?"

He said, "I killed my son."

"Mercy!" I thought. "How awful."

I arrived at the meeting place and I looked at the congregation. The hall was filled with sincere-looking men who were praying earnestly to God. Suddenly, I was gripped with a strong desire to set them free. I felt in my heart that these were good people who had repented of their mistakes. I wanted to rush to the main gate and command that the prisoners be set free.

It was then that I realized that I had no power to set these men free from prison. No matter what I thought and no matter how much money I had it would take a very, very high power to get them out of jail.

I thought of how difficult it would be to get a presidential pardon for the entire fellowship of murderers that attended my service.

They were in there for life and most of them would have to while away their time on earth in that prison.

That's when I realized how powerful the blood of Jesus was.

The Blood Redeems

We were bound in the devil's chains! We were drowning in our sins! We were guilty of all the charges! We were headed for Hell!

What could change our destiny? What could get us out of eternal prison? Only something extremely powerful could work out deliverance for you and me. After all, we are clearly guilty and there is no argument about that. The powerful thing with the ability to free us from our well-deserved prison is the blood of Jesus Christ. The blood of Jesus is the only thing with that kind of power. That is why we sing the song "What can wash away my sins; Nothing but the blood of Jesus! What can make me whole again? Nothing but the blood of Jesus!"

What has the power to save us from our wretched existence as prisoners? The King James Bible calls our wretched existence "our vain conversation".

2. **The blood of Jesus has the supernatural power to prevent death.**

    For the life of the flesh is in the blood: and I have given it to you upon the altar to make an atonement for your souls:

    Leviticus 17:11

The blood of Jesus has within it a supernatural ability to prevent death. The blood of Jesus has within it a supernatural ability to prevent you from going to Hell. Because the life is in the blood, the absence of life-giving blood causes death.

Medical science has discovered that any part of the human body that is deprived of blood dies.

For instance, sections of the brain tissue die when the blood supply to that section is blocked. This is what we call a stroke. Sections of the world are condemned to death when the blood of Jesus is stopped from flowing there. Entire regions of the world are condemned to death and Hell because no evangelist was able to go there. Life will come to many people when they receive the blood of Jesus.

The Leg Which Died

Years ago, I was in a consulting room of the hospital where I worked and my professor called me in to see a man whose leg was "dead". The man's leg had turned black and cold because the blood supply to the leg had been cut off in an accident.

This was the first time I had seen anything like that. I did not know that a section of the body could actually die and still be attached to the body. This man was in danger of developing gangrene in the dead leg, which would spread and kill him quickly. He had to have his leg amputated because the blood had stopped flowing to it. Just as the blood was prevented from flowing into a section of the man's body, the blood of Jesus is prevented from flowing to some sections of the world. These sections of the world are dominated by evil religions which put men in captivity and lead them to Hell.

That is why I am a preacher: to make the blood of Jesus avail for the souls of this world! I preach so that the blood of Jesus and the sacrifice of the cross will not be wasted. What praises we shall sing because of the great gift of salvation that we have through the blood of Jesus!

3. **The blood of Jesus has supernatural power to bring you back from the dead.**

    Now the God of peace, that BROUGHT AGAIN FROM THE DEAD our Lord Jesus, that great shepherd of the sheep, THROUGH THE BLOOD of the everlasting covenant,

    Hebrews 13:20

The Scripture teaches us that the blood of Jesus is the power that raised Jesus from the dead. The blood of Jesus has the power to raise the dead. It is the only power that could raise Jesus Christ out of the grave. It is by this same power of the blood that you will be raised from the dead. You will die, but you will not remain dead because of the power of the blood of Jesus.

The Man Who Vomited His Life Away

Blood has the power to bring back people from the dead. Even natural blood does that. That is why there are blood banks. These banks store blood so that blood can be accessed quickly in emergencies to bring people back to life.

One night, I was on duty at the emergency ward when a young man was brought to the hospital. This gentleman had an unusual problem in which he was vomiting blood. He retched and vomited all night long. Each time he vomited, it was bright red blood which came out. He never vomited a single morsel of food. His stomach was empty and he was bringing out pure blood. By 2.00am his condition began to deteriorate and I had to get blood for him.

I walked to and fro from the blood bank that night, fetching blood for this man. I was trying to bring him back from the dead. It was a race for life. By the morning the space around his bed was covered with bright red blood because he had vomited all around him all night long. Sad to say, in the end we were unable to prevent him from going to the grave because he had brought out more blood than we were able to replace.

The race that night was a race to get as much blood to the man quickly enough.

Only the blood could prevent the man from dying and going to the grave.

Indeed, the race today is the race to get the blood of Jesus to as many places as possible quickly enough. Only the blood of Jesus can prevent people from dying and going to Hell.

4. The blood of Jesus has the supernatural ability to open the gates of Heaven.

After this I beheld, and, lo, A GREAT MULTITUDE, which no man could number, of all nations, and kindreds, and people, and tongues, stood before the throne, and before the Lamb, clothed with white robes, and palms in their hands;

And cried with a loud voice, saying, Salvation to our God which sitteth upon the throne, and unto the Lamb....

And one of the elders answered, saying unto me, WHAT ARE THESE WHICH ARE ARRAYED IN WHITE ROBES? and whence came they? And I said unto him, Sir, thou knowest. And he said to me, THESE ARE THEY which came out of great tribulation, and HAVE WASHED THEIR ROBES, and made them white IN THE BLOOD OF THE LAMB.

Revelation 7:9-10, 13-14

Indeed, one of the wonders of Heaven is about how people like us could get into a place like Heaven?

How did we escape the prison we deserved to go to? How did we get out of the company of murderers and fellow fornicators?

How did we weave our way out of the sentence of death against us? How did we avoid the verdict of Hell?

Who do we know who made a way for us to come to Heaven? Which important person chipped in a word on our behalf? What are people like us doing in Heaven?

Where are our dirty clothes and filthy rags? How come we are dressed in white? Is this not a company of thieves, murderers and evil-doers?

How come they are singing hymns? How did people who hardly went to church manage to come to Heaven? Are they here on a visit? Are they going to be here forever?

But one of the elders has the answer. One of the elders explains that the multitudes have been able to come to Heaven by washing their robes in the blood of the lamb.

The Day I Entered the Anointed Car

One day, a great man of God visited our country. After the programme, thousands of people thronged him and a large security force had to help the man of God enter the waiting limousine. Everyone wanted to get a glimpse of the man of God or to touch the hem of his garment.

Eventually this man was whisked away by the driver and the host Bishop. Sitting in front of the car was one extra person. Who was this extra person and how did he get to be in the car when thousands of people just wanted to get a glimpse of him?

Who was the fourth man in the car? It was no other person than "yours truly"- myself! People always wondered how I got into such a privileged position. How did I enter the anointed car? I had the ride of a lifetime as well as a most important time of fellowship and impartation of the Spirit. It was a momentous occasion for me and I received a great anointing from one of God's generals just two weeks before he died. People asked, "How did you get into such a privileged and holy spot?" That's my secret.

Perhaps another question to ask is, "How did someone like you get into a church? How did someone like you become a minister of the gospel? What on earth is someone like you doing in a holy place?"

The only explanation that can be given for you and I to go to a place like Heaven will be the blood of Jesus. This incredibly great privilege is given to us by the blood of Jesus. One day I hope to stand in Heaven. Like everybody else I will be asked why the gates of Heaven should be opened to me. I do not hope to enter Heaven because I was a pastor or because I preached to large crowds. I hope to enter the gates of Heaven for the same reason as everybody else – the blood of Jesus! It is the blood of Jesus that we depend on for the opening of Heaven's gates.

5. The blood of Jesus has the supernatural power to overcome the devil.

And they OVERCAME HIM BY THE BLOOD OF THE LAMB, and by the word of their testimony; and they loved not their lives unto the death.

Revelation 12:11

The blood of Jesus has power. Through the blood of Jesus you will gain superiority over the devil and you will defeat him. Through the blood of Jesus you will win all the battles of life and ministry. Through the blood of Jesus you will deal with all the demonic problems of this world. It is time to overpower and overwhelm the devil through the powerful and precious everlasting blood of Jesus.

We live in a world dominated by an evil spirit of pride, rebellion and wickedness. This evil spirit is assisted by thousands of demons with the same evil character. All the struggles of our lives are related to the presence of evil spirits in the atmosphere. The atmosphere in different parts of the country and different parts of the world are determined by these evil spirits.

The Scripture has good news for us. We can overcome the devil and his cohorts. ⁷⁷We have been told exactly how we will overcome the devil – through the blood of Jesus.